Discovery Kids

Fluffy, Puffy ANIMALS

Written by Brenda Scott Royce

Silver Dolphin

PRE-LEVEL 1: ASPIRING READERS

 LEVEL 1: EARLY READERS

- Basic factual texts with familiar themes and content
- Concepts in text are reinforced by photos
- Includes glossary to reinforce reading comprehension
- Phonic regularity
- Simple sentence structure and repeated sentence patterns
- Easy vocabulary familiar to kindergarteners and first graders

 LEVEL 2: DEVELOPING READERS

 LEVEL 3: ENGAGED READERS

 LEVEL 4: FLUENT READERS

Silver Dolphin Books
An imprint of Printers Row Publishing Group
A division of Readerlink Distribution Services, LLC
9717 Pacific Heights Blvd, San Diego, CA 92121
www.silverdolphinbooks.com

Copyright © 2024 Printers Row Publishing Group. All rights reserved. Discovery Kids and all related elements © & ™ Warner Bros., Discovery, or its subsidiaries and affiliates.

No part of this publication may be reproduced, distributed, or transmitted in any form or by any means, including photocopying, recording, or other electronic or mechanical methods, without the prior written permission of the publisher, except in the case of brief quotations embodied in critical reviews and certain other noncommercial uses permitted by copyright law.

Printers Row Publishing Group is a division of Readerlink Distribution Services, LLC.
Silver Dolphin Books is a registered trademark of Readerlink Distribution Services, LLC.

All notations of errors or omissions should be addressed to Silver Dolphin Books, Editorial Department, at the above address.
ISBN: 978-1-6672-0831-2

All photography © iStock/Getty Images except for the following images: Hugh Lansdown/Shutterstock.com p. 25, Douglas Cliff/Shutterstock.com p. 26, armminivet/Shutterstock.com p. 32, Jack Pokoj/Shutterstock.com p. 63, Mariel Avalos p.95 top.

Every effort has been made to contact copyright holders for the images in this book. If you are the copyright holder of any uncredited image herein, please contact us at Silver Dolphin Books, 9717 Pacific Heights Blvd, San Diego, CA, 92121.
Manufactured, printed, and assembled in Heshan, China.
First printing, September 2024. LP/09/24
28 27 26 25 24 1 2 3 4 5

Contents

Baby Animals 5

Silly, Frilly, or Strange 37

Fluffy, Puffy Pets: Cats and Dogs 69

Fluffy, Puffy Hall of Fame 101

A NOTE TO PARENTS

Learning to read is an exciting time in your child's life! This book will help aspiring readers get started on their journeys.

All-Star Readers were created to help make learning to read a fun and engaging experience. Carefully selected stories and subject matter support the acquisition of reading skills, encourage children to learn about the world around them, and help develop a life-long love of books.

This Discovery Kids Level 1 collection offers fascinating factual content that is carefully crafted for new and developing readers. Every child is unique, and age or grade level does not determine a particular reading level.

As you read with your child, read for short periods of time and pause often. Encourage her to sound out words she does not know. Suggest she look at the picture on the page for clues about what the word might be. Have younger children turn the pages and point to pictures and familiar words. Each story in this book includes a glossary that defines new vocabulary words. When your child comes across a boldfaced word she doesn't recognize, instruct her to turn to the glossary and read its definition.

A good way to reinforce reading comprehension is to have a conversation about the book after finishing it. Children love talking about their favorite parts! As your child becomes a more independent reader, encourage him to discuss ideas and questions he may have.

Remember that there is no right or wrong way to share books with your child. When you find time to read with your child, you create a pattern of enjoying and exploring books that will become a love of reading!

Baby ANIMALS

Written by Brenda Scott Royce

Some animals are very fluffy when they are young.

Harp seal babies are born on ice. Thick, white fur keeps them warm.

The fur is like a built-in blanket. It absorbs the sun's rays and traps the warmth against the baby's body.

Grown-up seals have fat under their skin called **blubber**.

Blubber keeps seals warm in icy water.

Baby seals don't have blubber yet.

So, their thick coats are very important.

As a baby grows, it'll lose its white coat.

Then it'll be ready to swim in the sea.

For now, it stays on the ice . . . cozy under a blanket of fur.

Porcupines aren't always prickly. A newborn porcupine is fluffy! It is born with soft, bendy **quills**.

This baby won't stay fluffy for long. Its quills harden within a few days. Spiky quills protect the porcupine.

Baby cheetahs are fluffy too. These babies are called cubs.

Long, silvery hair grows along a cub's back.

The hair sticks up like a lion's mane.

A fluffy mane helps cheetah cubs hide.

It lets them blend in with tall, dry grass.

While their mom hunts, the cubs stay safely hidden.

In a few months, the cubs will grow big and strong.

Their long manes will disappear.

This fluffy baby is a dusky leaf monkey.

It has fuzzy orange hair.

The rest of the family is black, brown, or gray.

The baby's orange hair stands out. It helps the grown-ups look out for the baby.

Bit by bit, the baby loses its orange fur.

It is becoming **independent**.

A baby duck is called a duckling. Ducklings are fuzzy, but their parents are not.

When ducklings hatch, they are covered with **down**.

Down is a soft layer of fuzz.

Fuzzy ducklings can float and swim.

They can waddle and walk, but they cannot fly.

They must wait for their flying feathers to grow in.

Baby elephants are fuzzy too! They have patches of wiry hair.

Hair carries heat away from an elephant's skin.

This helps the baby stay cool in the hot sun.

Most monkeys live in warm places, like tropical rainforests.

Snub-nosed monkeys live high up in the mountaintops.
Here, winters are cold and long.

The baby snub-nosed monkey has long, silky hair.

This hair provides **insulation**.

It keeps the baby warm.

A tawny frogmouth chick looks like a cotton ball with a beak!

Soon it will grow speckled feathers.

These feathers help chicks blend in with trees.

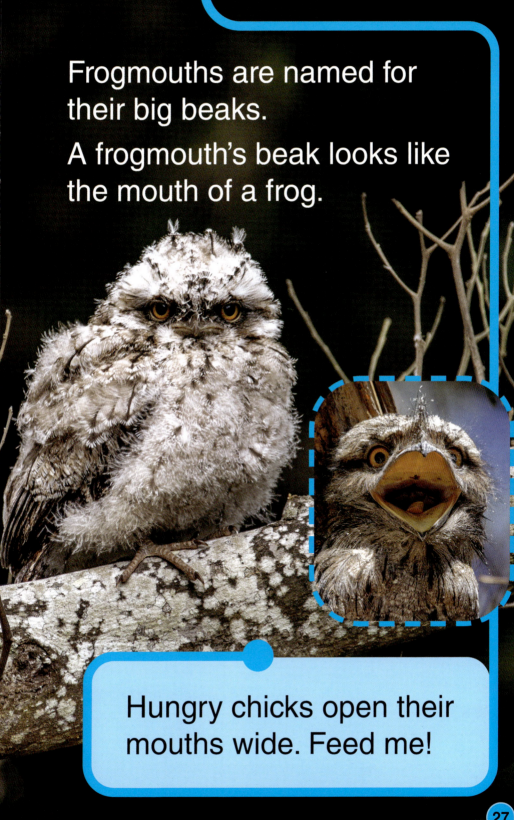

Frogmouths are named for their big beaks.

A frogmouth's beak looks like the mouth of a frog.

Hungry chicks open their mouths wide. Feed me!

Frogmouths have a neat trick. They pretend to be a tree branch. Can you see the chick's mom in this tree?

The chicks learn by watching their mother.

They practice freezing in place to blend into their surroundings.

Emperor penguins live near the South Pole.

These birds are built for the cold.

Thick feathers protect against water, wind, and ice.

A newly hatched chick is covered in down.

It needs help to keep warm.

Mom and Dad take turns carrying the chick on their feet.

It's cozy there, tucked beneath Mom's feathery belly.

Lots of penguins and their chicks live together in a **colony**.

The chick has grown bigger and fluffier.
It's time to make friends!

Giant pandas aren't giant when they are born.

A newborn panda is about the size of a stick of butter!

Pink and wrinkly, it doesn't look much like a panda.

Soon, the cub's fur grows in.

Now the cub has black and white markings, like its parents.

Baby pandas eat a lot.
Their bodies grow bigger . . . and rounder.
Look at that roly-poly baby!

A panda cub's fur is thick and woolly.

It keeps the cub warm.

Thick fur also acts like a cushion. It protects the cub if it tumbles or falls.

Glossary

blubber: a layer of fat that keeps animals warm

colony: a large group of animals that live together

down: thin, fluffy feathers that look like hair

independent: able to move around on its own

insulation: something that traps heat

quills: pointy spikes on a porcupine's body

Silly, Frilly, or STRANGE

Written by Brenda Scott Royce

Some animals may look a little silly or strange to us.

Let's meet some!

The axolotl is a type of salamander.

It has feathery fringes on the sides of its head.

The fringes are **gills**.

Gills pull oxygen out of the water.

They help the axolotl breathe.

Other salamanders change as they **mature**.
They lose their gills and live on land.

The axolotl gets bigger, but keeps its gills.

It needs them because it spends its whole life underwater.

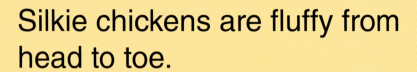

Silkie chickens are fluffy from head to toe.

They have puffy hairdos and feathers on their feet.

Other chickens have stiff feathers.
The silkie's feathers are soft.

Some people keep silkie chickens as pets.

Would you like a silkie as a pet?

A chipmunk looks silly when it stuffs its cheeks.

Pouches in the chipmunk's cheeks are like grocery bags.

It uses them to carry food.

It fills them with seeds and nuts to store and eat later.

A chipmunk's cheek pouches can stretch out to three times the size of its head.

Look at those puffy cheeks!

The mossy frog is great at **camouflage**.

These frogs live in damp forests.

Their skin looks like moss! It helps them blend into their surroundings.

Real moss is soft and springy. This frog's skin is bumpy and rough.

The secretary bird has a **crest** of feathers on its head.

It looks like a crazy crown!

The bird can lift or lower these feathers.

It will raise its crest when it hunts.

The secretary bird hunts a variety of animals, including snakes.

To its **prey**, this face may look scary!

This critter looks like a fuzzy worm.

It's a tiger moth caterpillar!

The tiger moth caterpillar spends its day snacking on plants.

It curls up when it gets scared.

It waits until the danger passes, then it uncurls and crawls away.

In spring, the caterpillar spins a **cocoon** around its body.

Then it transforms into a beautiful moth.

Many moths look furry. This helps keep them warm when they fly at night. A moth's "fur" is made of tiny scales.

To see a moth's fuzz, you have to look closely.

These pictures were taken by zooming in.

The Mangalica pig is unique. It's the world's only woolly pig.

These pigs look like sheep!

Its thick, curly hair keeps this pig cozy and warm.

The gelada monkey has very long, golden hair. It also has a patch of red skin on its chest.

These monkeys live in large troops.

Male geladas are much bigger than females.

The biggest male is the boss.

All that hair makes him look even bigger.

Jumping spiders are itsy-bitsy . . . and fuzzy-wuzzy.

The jumping spider has tiny hairs all over its body.

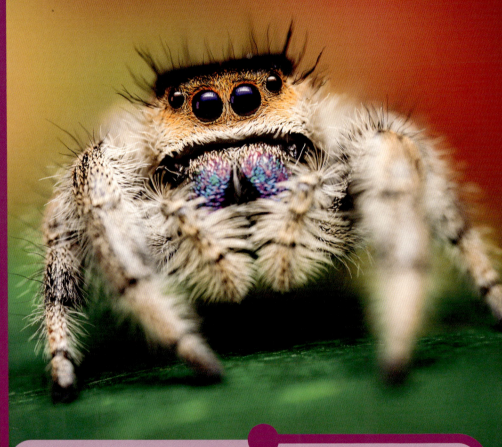

It has hairy **tufts** on its feet. The tufts act like sticky foot pads.

They cling to almost any surface. Being fuzzy helps the jumping spider climb walls.

The jumping spider hunts insects. It is harmless to people.

There are lots of silly, frilly creatures in the sea.

This animal looks like a puffy pom-pom.

It's a sea anemone.

Its frills are called **tentacles**.

They look silky, but they sting.

The sea anemone uses its tentacles to catch food.

Sea nettles have tentacles too.
A sea nettle is a type of jellyfish.

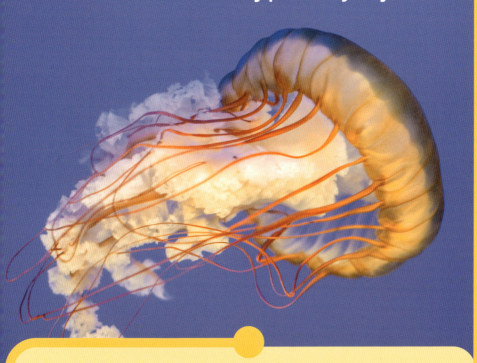

It has thick, frilly arms and long, thin tentacles.

Its arms hang from the center of its body.

Tentacles circle the outside.

Both its arms and its tentacles sting prey.

Who's that hairy-looking blob? It's a frogfish!

These fish are covered in spines that look like hair.

Frogfish "fish" for their dinner. They have a special spine that looks like a worm. They dangle it like bait.

When prey gets too close, the frogfish attacks.

Can you see a seahorse? Puffy polka dots would stand out anywhere else.

Here, they help the **pygmy** seahorse hide.

This type of seahorse can change its color.

It matches the coral where it lives.

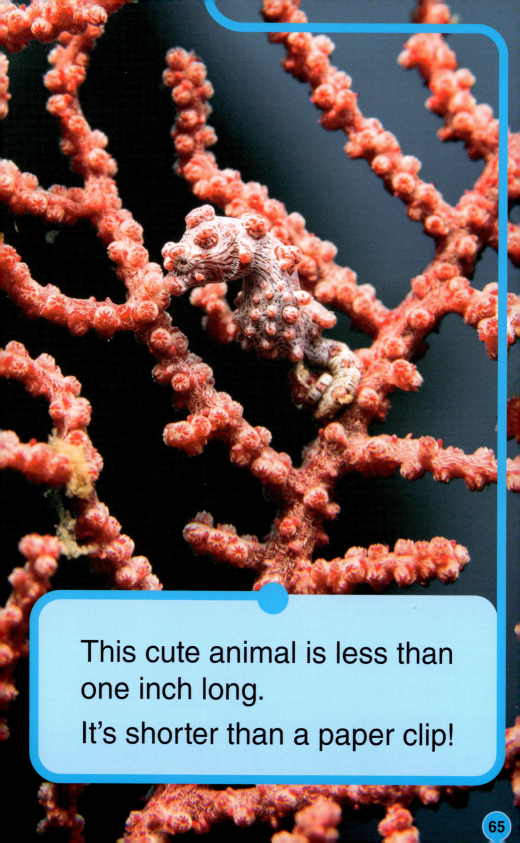

This cute animal is less than one inch long.

It's shorter than a paper clip!

The leafy sea dragon is also great at hiding.

Long frills on its body look like leaves.

They let this animal blend in with seaweed and other plants. It's the perfect disguise.

Being silly, frilly, or strange helps some animals survive!

Glossary

camouflage: when an animal blends in with its surroundings

cocoon: a silky covering that some insects make to protect themselves while they grow

crest: showy feathers on a bird's head

gills: body parts that help some animals breathe underwater

mature: to grow up or develop into an adult

prey: animals that are hunted by other animals for food

pygmy: a small type of animal

tentacles: long structures on some animals that are used for feeding or grasping

tufts: clusters of hair that stick out

Fluffy, Puffy Pets: CATS AND DOGS

Written by Brenda Scott Royce

Let's meet some of the planet's puffiest pets!

Persian cats come in many different colors.

Their hair is long and soft.
Their eyes are big and round.

Some people think Persians look grumpy.

Their faces can seem squished or scrunched.

They are sweet and gentle cats. Does this cat look grumpy to you?

Soft curls cover this cat's body.
It is a Selkirk Rex.
This **breed** is known for its curly fur.
Even its whiskers are wavy!

Selkirk Rex kittens are born with curly coats. The cuteness starts from day one.

The ragdoll cat's fur feels silky. These cats know how to relax.

Sometimes, they let their bodies go floppy . . . like a ragdoll.

That's how they got their name.

Maine coon cats are famously fluffy.

Their tails are long and bushy.

They have big paws with extra hair between their toes.

Most Maine coons have fluffy **tufts** on the tips of their ears.

Maine coon cats are the official cat of Maine!

The Siberian cat looks like a ball of fluff.

There's a big body underneath all that fur.

This cat can weigh up to 20 pounds.

That is heavier than a bowling ball!

The Norwegian forest cat looks wild, but it is **domestic**.

Its **ancestors** came from the forests of Norway.

These cats are also called Wedgies. A double coat protects this cat from cold and snow.

The lower layer is thick and woolly.
The outer layer is long and glossy.
If it gets wet, it can dry very quickly.

In hot summers, Wedgies don't need as much hair.

So they **shed** . . . a lot.

This little dog looks like a fluffy fox. It's a Pomeranian.

It has poofy hair and a pointy **muzzle**.

Its ears stand straight up.

These dogs are also called "Poms" or "Pom-Poms."

They are playful and have lots of energy.

The Afghan hound has the longest hair of any dog.

Afghans can grow up to three feet tall.

Their silky hair flows down to the ground.

It covers their ears and feet. Some Afghans have fancy hairdos.

This puffy dog is called a Puli. Its thick, shaggy coat keeps it warm.

Most Pulis are black or white.
Puli puppies have fine, wavy fur.
As their hair grows, it gets thicker.

It forms long, woolly cords that make the Puli look like a mop!

Their hair hangs over their eyes, but they can still see.

They even make great watchdogs.

The Samoyed was built for life in the snow.

Thick, white fur keeps it warm.

This dog's ancestors lived in the icy north.

They pulled sleds and guarded herds of reindeer.

Samoyeds are friendly, playful dogs.

Their upturned mouths make them look happy.

Their nickname is "smiling Sammy."

The Chow Chow looks like a giant teddy bear.

Its round face is very furry.

These dogs are strong and powerful.

They can weigh more than 60 pounds.

A Chow Chow's tongue is bluish-black.

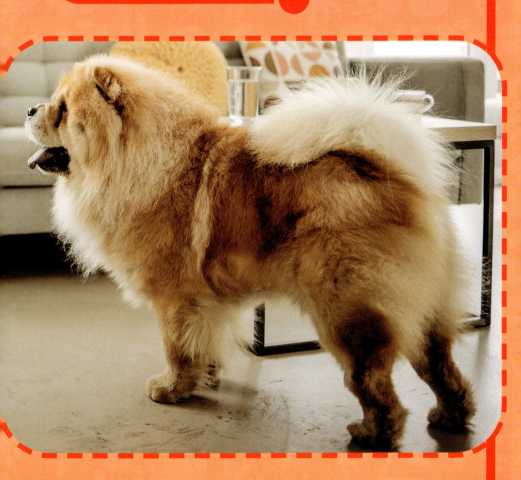

Its tail curls up over its back.

These small dogs have something in common.

Their coats are super silky and soft.

Their hair can grow very long.

Or it can be clipped short.

Mixed breed cats and dogs can be fluffy too.

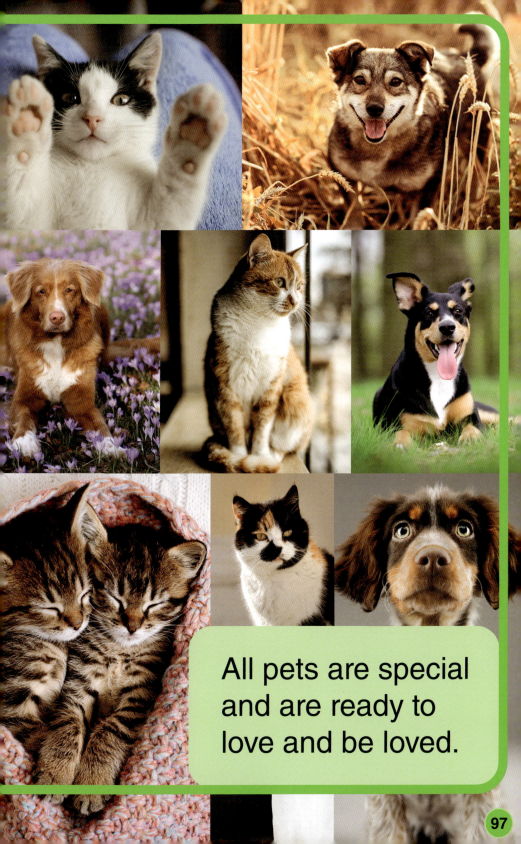

All pets are special and are ready to love and be loved.

All that fluffy fur needs extra care!

Grooming is a great way to spend time with your pet.

Be sure to comb out tangles and knots.

Brushing keeps a pet's coat clean and shiny.

They'll look so good they'll puff out with pride!

Glossary

ancestors: relatives that lived long ago

breed: an animal that shares similar features with other animals of the same type

domestic: an animal that lives with people instead of in the wild

grooming: cleaning, brushing, or combing a pet's fur

mixed breed: an animal that is more than one breed

muzzle: the nose and mouth of an animal, also called a "snout"

shed: to lose hair naturally

tufts: clusters of hair that stick out

Fluffy, Puffy HALL OF FAME

Written by Brenda Scott Royce

Best Slippers

Some animals are especially fluffy and puffy.

The red panda lives in the mountains.

Fluffy fur keeps it warm in cold weather.

A long, puffy tail helps it balance.

It even has fur on the bottoms of its feet . . . like built-in slippers.

Red pandas sleep in trees.

When it's cold, they curl up in a ball.

When it's hot, they dangle their legs over a branch.

King *of the* Mountain

The Pallas's cat is fluffy . . . and tough.

This wild cat lives in rocky mountains.

It is a great hunter.
Pallas's cats are about the size of a house cat.

Long, thick fur makes them look much bigger.
This helps protect them from **predators**.

Fuzziest Floater

The sea otter has the thickest fur of any animal.

Its fluffy fur traps tiny air bubbles next to the otter's skin.

All that air makes the otter float. It also keeps the otter's skin warm and dry.

Sea otters spend half their day **grooming**.

They lick their fur to keep it clean.

They rub it with their paws. They even blow air into their fur to fluff it up.

Super Soaker

When the weather gets colder, the Japanese macaque's fur grows thicker.

This **species** is also called a "snow monkey."

Snow monkeys huddle together to share body heat.

They have another way to warm up.
They take a bath in a hot spring!

The water here is warm.
It is like soaking in a hot tub!

Color-Change Champ

The snowshoe hare has a brown coat in summer.

Its brown coat blends in with trees and grass.

It has a white coat in winter. The white coat helps the hare hide in snow.

The hare's white winter coat is extra fluffy for warmth.

The snowshoe hare was named for its feet.

Snowshoes help people walk on top of snow.

The snowshoe hare's feet are extra big and covered with stiff fur.

They let the hare hop across snow without sinking.

Great Inflator

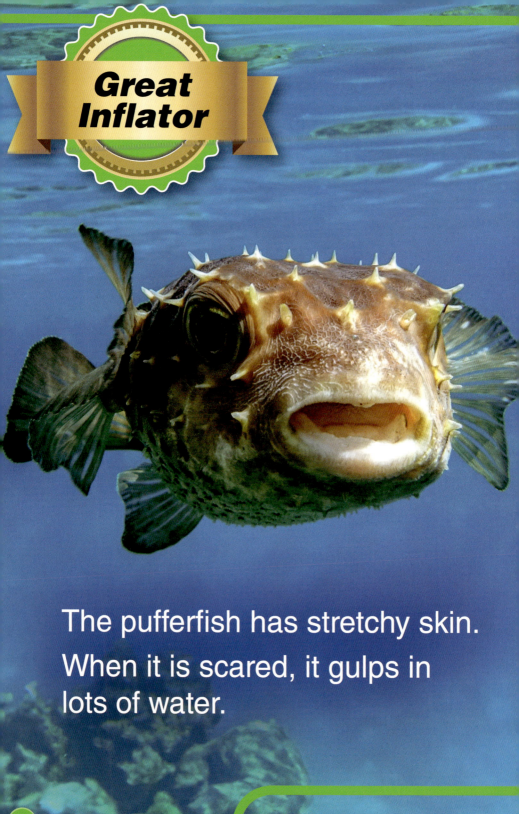

The pufferfish has stretchy skin. When it is scared, it gulps in lots of water.

Poof!

It puffs up like a balloon.

Spikes on its skin stand out.

Predators are scared to come near the fish.

Being puffy keeps the pufferfish safe!

Cutest Curler

A hedgehog's body is covered with **quills**.

Its belly is very soft.

If it sees a predator, the hedgehog curls into a ball.

It lifts up its quills.

It looks like a spiky ball.

The quills protect the hedgehog from danger.

Softest Fur

The chinchilla may be the world's softest animal.

Its fur has a silky, smooth **texture**. Each strand of its hair is super thin.

Fifty or more hairs grow out of a single **follicle**.

All that hair makes the chinchilla fluffy and soft.

Woolly Winner

Look at these fluffy faces!
Alpacas belong to the camel family.

They are famous for their soft coats.

Their wool is used to make sweaters and blankets.

Sweetest Smile

The quokka is fluffy and looks like it's smiling!

The quokka lives in Australia. It is related to the kangaroo.

Top Locks

A lionhead rabbit has a ruffle of fur around its neck.

It looks like a lion's mane!

Some guinea pigs have really long hair.

This one has long hair that never stops growing!

Best in Snow

The arctic fox lives in the **tundra**. It's a place that is frozen for most of the year.

A bushy tail keeps this fox snug and warm while it sleeps.

It curls its tail around its body like a scarf.

Good night!

Glossary

follicle: a hole on skin out of which hair grows

grooming: cleaning an animal's fur

predators: animals that eat other animals for food

quills: pointy spikes on the body of some animals

species: a type of animal that shares the same features

texture: how something feels when it is touched

tundra: a treeless area where the ground is usually frozen